Saving Seal

the plastic predicament

DIANE JACKSON HILL

Illustrated by

CRAIG SMITH

MUSEUMSVICTORIA
PUBLISHING

Lizzie lived in the city but spent most summer holidays with her grandpa on *The Eagle*.

Grandpa Dave was a marine biologist and had sailed his boat around the world, exploring ocean currents and marine life. Now he helped care for the Bay.

The Eagle had everything
Lizzie needed.

A bunk bed
with a porthole,

a dishwasher,
a milkshake-maker

and even an
occasional visitor.

Seal was an old friend of Lizzie's. Every year he'd be there in the Bay—resting on the rock ledges or wharf, skylarking when the waters were still, or teasing fishermen.

He'd watch the fishermen reel in their lines
then chomp off the tails of their fish.

He'd throw his catch into the air and devour it in one gulp.

Seal was a show-off, but sometimes he caught more than fish.

One day,
Lizzie spotted
Seal close by.

He was **thrashing** against the rocks
and **twisting** his tail flippers.

'GRANDPA!

Seal is all knotted up.'

Grandpa Dave scrambled for his net and threw it over Seal to keep him still. 'Seal has been playing with an old plastic bag,' he said, while cutting his flippers free.

'There's so much rubbish around the Bay. One wave washes it out to sea, and the next wave dumps it all back.'

That night Lizzie dreamed she was Seal, swimming in the ocean.

But something wasn't right: she couldn't kick her legs and it was getting harder to swim.

Lizzie woke in a sweat.

She was tangled in her sheet the way Seal had been tangled in the plastic bag.

‘We have to do something, Grandpa. Seal loves to play around here, but it’s not safe for him now.’

‘If we could work out where all the rubbish comes from,’ Grandpa Dave said, ‘we may be able to stop it clogging up the Bay.’ To Lizzie, that sounded like a plan.

Lizzie and Grandpa Dave began collecting rubbish from the water and shores of the Bay. Lizzie loved being organised so Grandpa Dave gave her the task of sorting, counting and recording the rubbish they found.

Grandpa Dave and Lizzie combed the beach and scoured the shallows. They collected…

But when they came back to the boat…

'**GRANDPA**, Seal has something caught in his nose.'

Grandpa Dave threw his net over Seal, and eased out a plastic straw.

That night, when Lizzie drank her strawberry milkshake, she was glad Grandpa had paper straws.

When they searched under the wharf

they gathered up…

But back on the boat…

‘**GRANDPA**, this time it’s old balloons and ribbons.’

Grandpa Dave threw his net over Seal. Lizzie carefully clipped the ties while Grandpa tugged at the tangles.

Each day, they left their patch clean.

But it didn't stay that way.

After Lizzie had finished her long list,

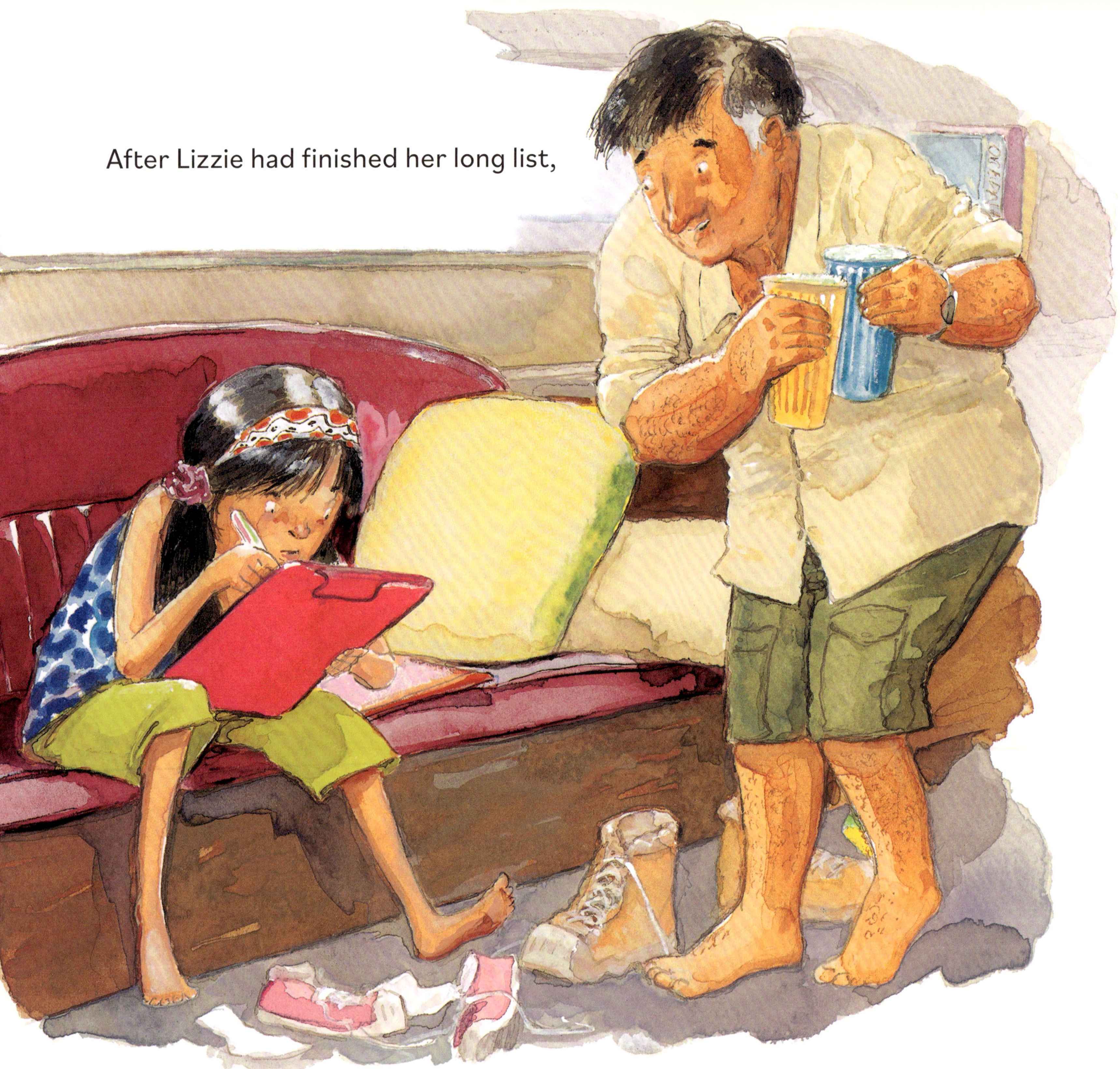

both she and Grandpa needed a spearmint milkshake.

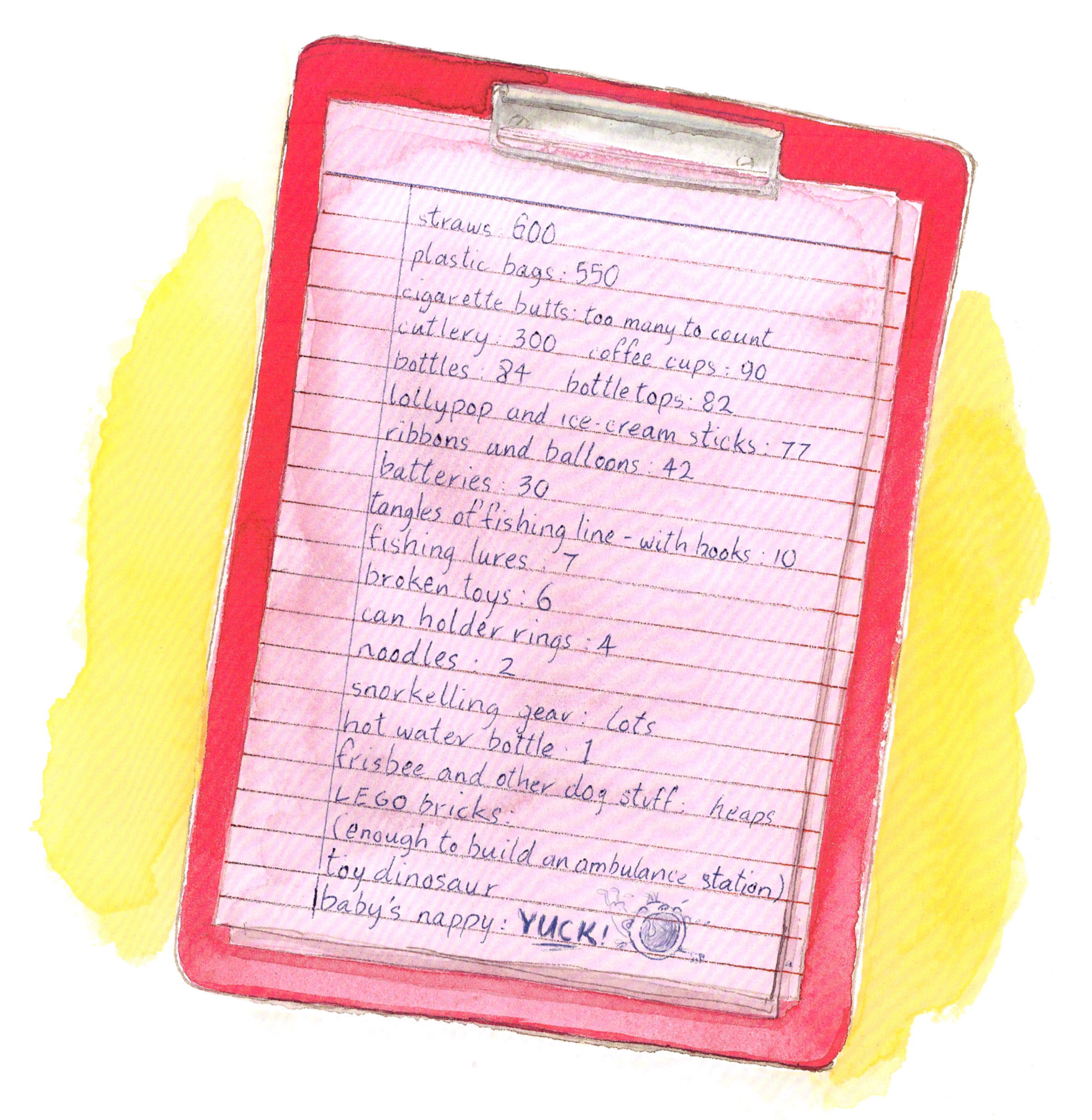

They didn't worry about a straw.

Lizzie and Grandpa Dave had
the facts and figures now.
'Let's go tell everyone,' said Lizzie.

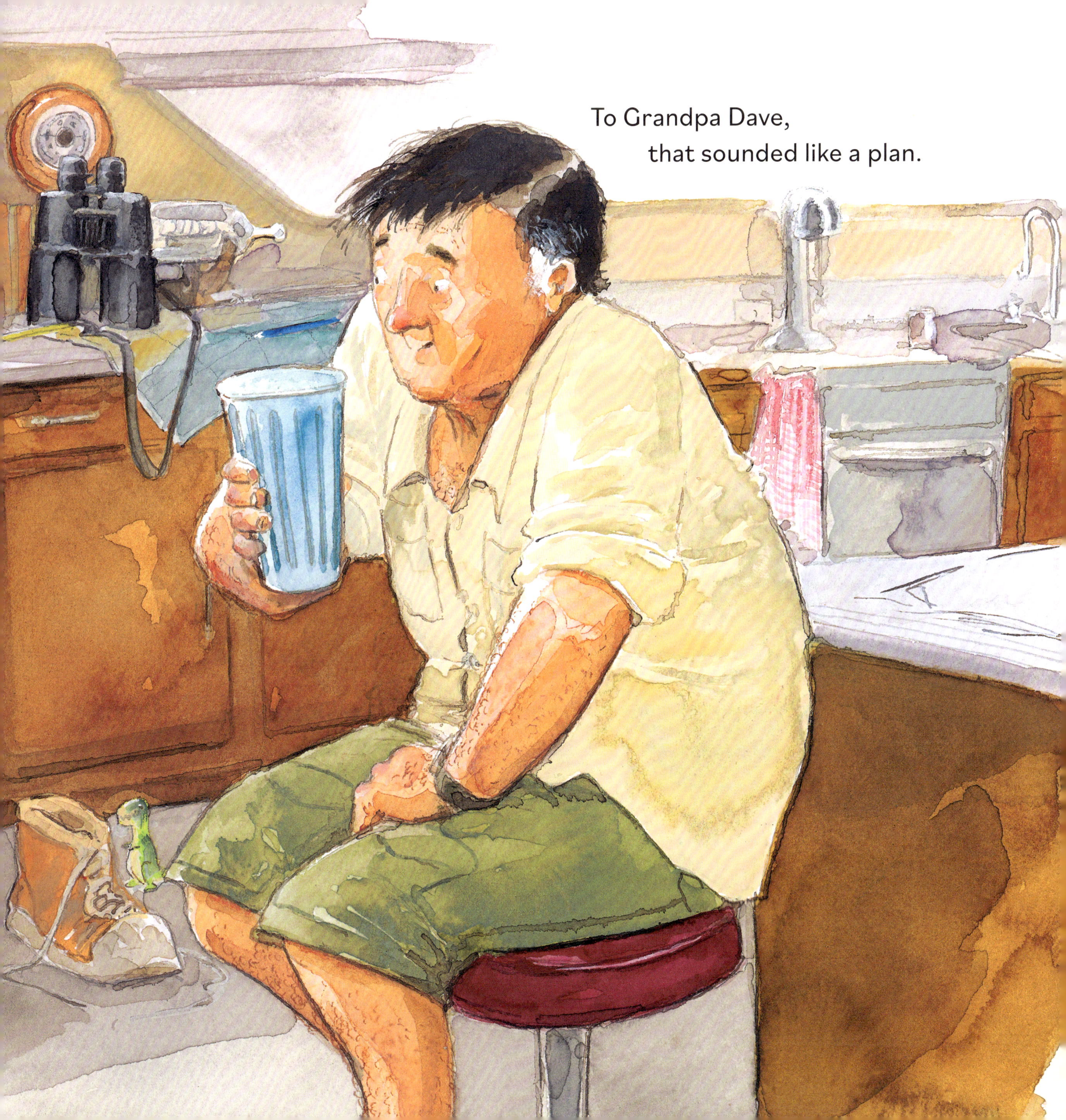

To Grandpa Dave,
that sounded like a plan.

When Lizzie and Grandpa Dave took their facts and figures to their local council and shopkeepers, all sorts of things happened in the town.

Single-use plastics, including plastic bags and straws, were banned.

Volunteers made cloth bags for shoppers who forgot to bring their own.

Everyone started using their own water bottles and coffee cups.

More bins were placed along the beach and near the wharf. Beach clean-ups were organised.

It took a few years but with the help of newspaper and TV reports, and social media, the clean-up message about the plastic predicament spread from one bay to the next…

and the next…

It had been many years since Lizzie spent summer holidays on *The Eagle*, but she was visiting one day when…

'GRANDPAAAAAAA…'

'What's up with Seal?'
yelled Grandpa Dave,
as he scrambled for his net.

'Seal's okay, Grandpa. **LOOK!**'

The Problem With Plastic

Scientists believe that if we don't act now, in thirty years time there will be more plastic in the ocean than fish!

Millions of tons of plastic ends up in our oceans every year and most of it comes from people throwing away used plastic on our streets, near our rivers and on our beaches. It then travels by rain or wind or currents and ends up in our oceans.

Plastic takes hundreds of years to decompose. Before it does, it may entangle marine life. And as it does break down, it becomes a soup of tiny particles which smell and look like food. This is eaten by seabirds and marine life.

Plastics and their toxins harm marine life and can also be passed on to us in our food.